BUDGIES

BEGI

Complete guide on everything you need to know about your budgies: food, care, health, lifespan, breeding and Dealing with your budgies

James Anthony

Table of Contents

CHAPTER ONE 3

   INTRODUCTION...3

CHAPTER TWO 7

   SETTING UP 7

CHAPTER THREE 11

   TAKING CARE OF BUDGIES...........................11

CHAPTER FOUR 16

   HEALTH 16

CHAPTER FIVE 20

   CARE..20

INTRODUCTION

budgies are one of the most well known partners with their striking shading, bringing dynamic quality and character into your family. Make the ideal home for your new pet budgie with this accommodating aide.

Budgie reality document

Life expectancy – Up to 10 years

Size – Up to 18cm

Diet – Birdseed, pellets, verdant green veggies and new natural product

Home – 31cm x 46cm x 46cm enclosure

Care and upkeep

Budgies can remember many words and learn different stunts. They can live for as long as 10 years and are known for being chatty pets. As bringing a budgie home is a genuine responsibility, here are some key things you have to consider before getting one:

1. Do you have fitting lodging for your budgie?

2. Can you give a sheltered domain to them?

3. Can you give day by day directed time outside of the enclosure for your budgie?

4. Are you mindful that fowls can be vocal and have you checked this is adequate to your family and neighbors?

A solid budgie ought to have spotless and smooth plumes, a ready and upstanding stance, clear and standard breathing and no release around their snout, eyes, or ears. In case you're a first-time budgie parent, you may just need to begin with one new winged creature. However, budgies are profoundly social and will show an extraordinary reaction in the event that they have an accomplice. On the off chance that budgies fly solo for significant stretches of time they can turn out to be forlorn and discouraged. Having a friend will keep them upbeat – and a glad flying creature implies a solid fowl.

CHAPTER TWO

SETTING UP

You should pick a sufficiently estimated confine for your budgie relying upon how much space you have accessible and the quantity of feathered creatures you need to assemble. Your budgie's confine or aviary should give them space to spread their wings – they love to loosen up. Along these lines, we suggest a rectangular confine.

Your pet will require paper at the base of their pen. This will let you screen the number, size, shading and consistency of the droppings. In the event that you are wanting to raise your fowls, you can discover settling material that your budgie will adore at your nearby Petbarn. Budgies like to be perfect so try to look at for and clean defecation or droppings in your pen week by week. You ought to likewise change the paper at the base of the confine every day and clean roosts week after week.

Put a bowl in their pen with the goal that your budgie can wash when they please. Budgies are dynamic and curious feathered creatures, so they need an assortment of toys to hold their consideration and fight off weariness. Your budgie's home ought to incorporate loads of roosts, swings and intuitive components to animate their faculties. Budgies likewise love reflected surfaces and shreddable toys.

Spot the confine at or underneath eye level, away from over the top daylight and away from anything that is very fragrant, similar to those scents found in the kitchen. Fowls have a proficient respiratory framework. They ingest anything noticeable all around truly well and effectively experience the ill effects of things like mist concentrates, tobacco smoke, fundamental oils, and so on.

CHAPTER THREE

TAKING CARE OF BUDGIES

Pellets make a decent base eating routine for budgies, so ensure that you revive the pellet bowl every day. Verdant greens give basic nutrients and minerals and can be given to them each other day. Your budgie ought to have organic products just once per week and treats are best given just once month to month. What's more, giving your budgie a bit of cuttlefish is extraordinary for their nose and will likewise support their calcium levels.

Never feed your budgie chocolate, lettuce, avocado, rhubarb, liquor, natural product seeds or caffeine as they can make your pet wiped out. In the event that your budgie hasn't eaten the natural product or vegetables in 24 hours, ensure you evacuate it and supplant with new food.

Give a water dish to your flying creature so they approach drinking water consistently. Wash the water bowl out in lathery water or put it through the dishwasher. They may get a kick out of the chance to wash in water dishes, so it's essential to watch that their water bowl is full and new frequently. Try not to put your budgie's water bowl underneath their roost as they can pollute it.

Voyaging

The most ideal approach to ship your budgie is in a little, secured confine, pet transporter or even a little box. The size ought not be smothering, yet sufficiently huge for your pet to be agreeable. Leave any sharp articles or unstable things at home to forestall your budgie being harmed. A couple of safely fixed bars is sufficient for them to appreciate the ride.

Secure the pen with a seat strap. For long excursions, you may need to shield the enclosure from direct daylight and make water stops to keep your pet hydrated and agreeable.

Prepping

Budgies will prep themselves consistently. In the event that your budgie is healthy, you'll notice them cleaning their quills, scratching their bill on different surfaces around the confine and in any event, having a shower.

You'll despite everything need to cut your budgie's nails occasionally. Their plumes may should be cut as well; this can be hazardous whenever done inaccurately. For proficient direction, allude to your nearby Greencross Vets.

CHAPTER FOUR

HEALTH

Budgie medicinal services is about counteraction. They are inclined to contracting parasites, similar to worms or lice, and can have respiratory issues and stomach related issues. Be that as it may, on the off chance that they are singular pets, at that point there are less possibilities for them to get worms or lice. Respiratory sicknesses can be dodged by taking care of them right and keeping them in a spotless region.

To evade any medical problems, you have to check your pet

feathered creature for worms or lice and look for treatment in the event that they have any parasites. Except if there are different winged animals traveling every which way constantly there is little danger of contracting worms.

It's imperative to watch out for your budgie's wellbeing. Check them regularly for signs, for example, lightened up quills, shut eyes, torpidity, slouched pose, hanging tail or wings, release around the eyes, nose or mouth, wheezing and hacking, looseness of the bowels and sporadic relaxing.

1. If you notice any of these signs, or whatever else particular about your budgie's appearance or conduct, allude to your neighborhood Greencross Vets for treatment and counsel. A decent offset diet with no unexpected changes

2. Plenty of toys to keep them interested

3. Water jug and feed bowls cleaned every day

4. Their nails cut a few times each year – approach your vet for exhortation

5. A day by day shower – basic for their dressing exercises

6. Regular practice outside their confine

CHAPTER FIVE

CARE

It's alright to let your budgie out of their enclosure from time to time. It might be suitable to take away their freedom if your winged animal hasn't been hand restrained so they don't get injured flying into windows or furniture.

When letting your pet out of their fenced in area, it's essential to watch out for them. The best arrangement is to keep any potential perils off the beaten path and screen them cautiously.

Tip: Birds have delicate respiratory frameworks. Scented candles, deodorizers and aromas can hurt them.

Budgie agenda

Petbarn has all the fledgling supplies you requirement for your new pet budgie on the web and coming up.

Lodging

1. Cage

2. Perch

3. Water bowl

4. Bathing bowl

5. Food

6. Bird pellets

7. Fruits sporadically

8. Seeds

9. Vegetables

Exercise and Entertainment:

Budgies are insightful and curious feathered creatures that appreciate playing and climbing. Toys are basic to invigorate them intellectually and genuinely – particularly significant for winged creatures kept all alone. Budgies can likewise be instructed to copy sounds and talk. In the event that they hear similar words more than once from a similar individual they may get them and start imitating the words or expressions. A single fowl will require more consideration and love than a couple or gathering and ought to be dealt with consistently.

Dealing with:

With tolerance, Budgies can turn out to be very agreeable in spite of the fact that it is fundamental they are prepared since the beginning, and by one individual in particular. The initial step is to get the fowl used to being stroked inside its enclosure – utilize a stick or roost, not your hands. Start by delicately stroking its chest two or three times each day, at that point urge it to hop onto the stick. Next, rehash the entire procedure through the entryway of the enclosure as opposed to the bars. At long last, rehash, utilizing your hands this time rather than the stick. This is a slow procedure that may take half a month however for the most part works at long last.

To get your Budgie, guarantee your palm covers its back and wings while your center and pointer encompass the flying creature's neck. Be delicate – Budgies will nibble on the off chance that they feel pushed. On the off chance that getting an aviary fledgling utilize a cushioned edge net and never attempt to get it in mid flight - consistently hold up until it is roosted securely.

Reproducing:

Budgies can be mated from about a year old and will create a grip of 4-6 eggs in around 18-21 days. Similarly as with all pets, rearing Budgies requires a lot of duty of time and exertion. It is suggested that you in this way look for master counsel and do proper exploration before considering keeping a rearing pair and just in case you're sure you can discover great homes for the children.

Printed in Great Britain
by Amazon